Y0-DWP-744

MEASURING VOLCANIC ACTIVITY

Follow the Clues

by Jennifer Zeiger

CHERRY LAKE PUBLISHING · ANN ARBOR, MICHIGAN

CHERRY LAKE
Publishing

Published in the United States of America by Cherry Lake Publishing
Ann Arbor, Michigan
www.cherrylakepublishing.com

CONTENT ADVISER: Melissa Miller, Next Generation Science Standards Writer, Science Teacher, Farmington, Arkansas

PHOTO CREDITS: Cover and page 1, U.S. Geological Survey / tinyurl.com/lrs8hq7 / CC-BY-2.0; page 4, © SergiyN/Shutterstock.com; page 5, © www.sandatlas.org/ Shutterstock.com; page 6, © Elena Kalistratova/Shutterstock.com; page 7, © Estivillml/Dreamstime.com; page 8, © Maridav/Shutterstock.com; page 9, © John Elk III/Alamy; page 10, © Bryan Lowry/Alamy; page 11, © Mary Terriberry/ Shutterstock.com; page 12, © Dave G. Houser/Alamy; page 13, © Craig Ellenwood/ Alamy; page 14, © imageBROKER/Alamy; page 15, © National Geographic Image Collection/Alamy; page 16, © wavebreakmedia/Shutterstock.com; page 17, © Paul Laubach 3rd/Shutterstock.com; page 18, © Vadim Petrakov/Shutterstock.com; page 19, © Goodluz/Shutterstock.com; page 20, © Stocktrek Images, Inc./Alamy; page 21, © M Stock/Alamy; page 22, © RZ Design/Shutterstock.com; page 23, © Fredy Thuerig/Shutterstock.com; page 24, © Benjamin Simeneta/Shutterstock. com; page 25, © Zach Holmes/Alamy; page 26, © epa european pressphoto agency b.v./Alamy; page 27, © KPG Payless2/Shutterstock.com; page 28, © Jeff Whyte/Shutterstock.com; page 29, © Teemu Tretjakov/Shutterstock.com.

LIBRARY OF CONGRESS CATALOGING-IN-PUBLICATION DATA
Zeiger, Jennifer, author.
  Measuring volcanic activity / by Jennifer Zeiger.
    pages cm. — (Science explorer) (Follow the clues)
  Summary: "Find out how scientists measure volcanic activity by following along with this exciting story." —Provided by publisher.
  Audience: Grades 4 to 6.
  Includes bibliographical references and index.
  ISBN 978-1-63362-389-7 (lib. bdg.) — ISBN 978-1-63362-417-7 (pbk.) — ISBN 978-1-63362-473-3 (e-book) —ISBN 978-1-63362-445-0 (pdf)
  1. Volcanoes—Juvenile literature. 2. Volcanism—Juvenile literature. 3. Volcanic activity prediction—Juvenile literature. I. Title.
  QE521.3.Z45 2016
  551.21—dc23   2014045951

Cherry Lake Publishing would like to acknowledge the work of the Partnership for 21st Century Skills. Please visit *www.p21.org* for more information.

Printed in the United States of America, Corporate Graphics Inc.
July 2015

TABLE OF CONTENTS

CHAPTER 1

VOLCANIC VACATION

Hawai'i is famous for its beautiful natural landscapes.

Shawn helped his aunt and cousins unload his luggage from their truck. He was visiting them in Hawai'i for the first time. He couldn't wait to see Hawai'i's beautiful beaches! He also wanted to hear more about his aunt April's job as a **volcanologist** at the Hawaiian Volcano **Observatory** (HVO).

While they were bringing the bags inside, Shawn's older cousin, Reggie, asked, "Did you see the volcano when you flew over, Shawn?"

"Volcano?" Shawn dropped the backpack he was carrying on the living room floor. Suddenly he was scared. "Is there really a volcano, Aunt April?"

Reggie's little sister, Kayla, spoke up before April could answer. "Yup!" she shouted excitedly. "And it's erupting!"

Shawn's eyes widened. "But isn't that dangerous?"

"Volcanoes are certainly dangerous," April answered. "But that doesn't necessarily mean we're in danger here. How much do you know about volcanoes?"

"A little," Shawn responded. "I know that volcanoes are places where **magma** from deep underground comes up to the surface. Once magma reaches the surface, it's called lava."

April nodded. "Hot gases come from volcanoes, too. Really powerful eruptions might shoot solid bits of rock and ash into the air. But

↰ Lava is extremely hot.

sometimes lava flows more gently out of an opening in the earth's crust. That's what volcanoes usually do here in Hawai'i."

"Even then, the lava's really hot and very dangerous," Reggie pointed out. "You should still stay away from it."

"So how do I know if I'm in danger when a volcano erupts?" asked Shawn.

"Monitor it," explained April. "That is part of what we do at the volcano observatory."

"How do you monitor a volcano?"

"A few different ways," April said. "We set up some equipment on the ground. It records movements in the earth, changes in the water, and gases in the air. It uses cameras to take photos and videos, too. We also use

Volcanoes sometimes shoot clouds of ash and smoke into the air when they erupt.

Puʻu ʻŌʻō has been erupting nonstop since 1983.

satellites in space to gather information. All of these measurements help us predict when and how a volcano might erupt."

Shawn still looked nervous. "How does that work?"

"Kīlauea is erupting now. Why don't we use that as an example?" Reggie suggested. "Lava erupts from a lot of places on Kīlauea, but we could focus on the **lava flow** from Puʻu ʻŌʻō **crater**. That's what people are really watching closely right now. We can try to figure out how big a threat the eruption is ourselves."

"That's a great idea!" Kayla said with a grin.

"Absolutely," said April. "But first, let's get Shawn settled and have some dinner."

"Yes!" exclaimed Kayla. "I'm starving."

HISTORY'S DEADLIEST VOLCANOES

Kīlauea's eruptions are usually peaceful enough for tourists to get a close look at them.

Kīlauea is one of the most active volcanoes in the world, but it is not the most destructive. It often erupts fairly quietly. Lava oozes from **vents** or shoots out in a fountain.

Other volcanoes are more likely to suffer violent explosions. Mount Vesuvius is one famous example. In 79 CE, it erupted with unexpected power. Pompeii, Stabiae, and other nearby cities were buried under volcanic ash and rock.

The volcano Krakatau shook Indonesia in 1883 with an eruption loud enough to be heard in Australia. Earthquakes, hot ash and lava, and **tsunamis** created by the event killed more than 36,000 people.

The deadliest eruption in history occurred in Indonesia less than 70 years before Krakatau. In 1815, Mount Tambora sent so much ash into the air that it blocked the sun for days. About 10,000 people died during the eruption itself. The massive amounts of ash that filled the air and settled on the land also ruined the year's crops. Historians estimate that another 80,000 people died of starvation as a result.

CHAPTER 2

MEETING THE VOLCANO

Visitors to the Thomas A. Jaggar Museum can watch a volcano eruption in person.

The next day, April had an announcement. "Let's drive out to the Thomas A. Jaggar Museum today. It has lots of information on volcanoes. There's also an overlook where you can see one of Kīlauea's vents. It's not Puʻu ʻŌʻō but at least you'll be able to see Kīlauea in action."

Shawn was excited. "Let's start there after lunch. We'll see Kīlauea and learn about volcanoes at the museum. Then we can come back here and use the Internet to gather more data on the eruption."

"Great plan!" April said.

The family piled into April's truck a few hours later. The drive was not long, and the view along the way was very pretty. However, it was nothing compared to the view they got once they reached the overlook. Across a rocky area, a long column of steam rose from a pit. At the base of the steam was an orange glow.

"That glow comes from the lava," Kayla said, pointing.

Reggie joined them at the railing. "The smoke carries gases into the air. Scientists like Mom keep an eye on them. Some gases, such as sulfur dioxide and carbon dioxide, can be dangerous."

An erupting volcano is a beautiful sight.

Acid rain damages trees and other plant life.

"What does sulfur dioxide do?" Shawn asked.

"It can make it hard to breathe, especially if you are already sick," April explained. "If there is a lot of it, it might make your eyes burn or even cause **acid rain**."

"It also smells really bad," Kayla said.

"It certainly does," agreed April. "But there's not enough of it coming from that vent to worry about." She pointed to the Jaggar Museum building behind them. "Let's spend some time inside and learn about this volcano. Later on, when it's getting dark, you'll be able to see what the volcano really looks like."

The Jaggar Museum is filled with informative exhibits about volcanology.

Everyone filed into the museum. Kayla went straight to her favorite exhibit: old volcanologist gear. Shawn went through the museum more slowly. He wanted to learn as much as possible. Reggie helped explain things along the way.

"Volcanoes created the Hawaiian Islands, see?" he said, pointing to an illustration. "Lava cooled down and turned into rock. Then it built up, spread out, and created the land we're standing on."

He showed Shawn a **seismograph**. "These machines record movements in the earth. Little rumbles cause the wire to move just a little bit across the paper. You probably won't feel those rumbles. Bigger earthquakes register as wider marks."

"What does that have to do with a volcano?" Shawn asked.

"Sometimes earthquakes happen just before a volcano erupts," Reggie explained. "Magma builds up under the earth, building pressure. The pressure makes the earth shake. Earthquakes might start days or even months before the eruption. If experts notice a series of quakes and think an eruption might occur, they can tell people nearby to **evacuate**."

Scientists rely on seismographs to measure the strength of volcano-related earthquakes.

"Which saves lives," Shawn guessed.

"Exactly. Especially if the eruption is explosive, which often happens when there are earthquakes."

Just then, Kayla came running up to them. "Closing! Closing!"

April quickly caught up to her. "Hey," she said. "No running, Kayla. It is near closing time, though," she added, turning to Reggie and Shawn. "Why don't we go outside?"

It was still light out when they walked up to the overlook. However, time went by quickly, and Shawn watched the sky darken. As the sun went down, the orange glow in the crater seemed to become much brighter. He smiled. "This is beautiful!"

A volcanic eruption lights up the night sky in shades of orange and yellow.

WATCHING VOLCANOES

Studying volcanoes up close can be dangerous work.

Many volcano observations can be done from a distance. Seismographs and other instruments are placed at the volcano, but their data can be accessed from anywhere. As a result, volcanologists might spend much of their time at laboratories far from the volcanoes they study. This keeps them safe from potentially dangerous eruptions. It also provides a place for them to look at samples, create models, write about their findings, and do other work that requires a computer or a desk.

More exciting work takes place when volcanologists venture out into the field. They do this to take samples, chart the landscape, and explore a volcano in person. Often, this means traveling to places that are difficult to reach. The scientists might climb tall mountains or dive under the ocean. Some volcanoes can only be reached by helicopter, by boat, or on foot. And if a volcano is erupting—or about to erupt—volcanologists have to be extra careful to protect themselves. Sometimes, sturdy boots, pants, and long sleeves will do. Masks provide protection from harmful gases. If an eruption is particularly dangerous, scientists might need to wear special heat suits.

Writing things down in a notebook is one of the simplest ways to organize ideas and plan out a project.

When the family returned home that evening, Shawn grabbed a pencil and a notebook from his bag. "Now I know more about volcanoes in general. So what's the next step?" he asked. "How do we figure out if the eruption at Puʻu ʻŌʻō will put us in danger?"

"We should gather information on the eruption," April said. "HVO posts updates about it on its Web site. We can also pull some data directly from HVO instruments and computers. Then we'll analyze our data and

compare it to what has happened in the past. That will help us predict what might happen in the near future."

"Let's get cracking!" Kayla jumped to the computer. She went straight to the Kīlauea info on HVO's Web site.

They began by making a chart of the earthquake activity during the Pu'u 'Ō'ō eruption. Then they charted the different gases that had come from the lava flow. Shawn noticed that the biggest numbers on that chart belonged to water **vapor** and sulfur dioxide.

"We don't worry too much about water vapor," April explained. "Sulfur dioxide is our main threat here. It's good to keep track of it."

↖ Some gases from volcanic eruptions are more dangerous than others.

Shawn also wrote down how far the lava flow had traveled over the last two months and how much area it covered. He did some math to figure out how fast the lava spread each day. April checked his work and compared it to what the HVO scientists estimated.

"There are big differences in the lava's speed from day to day," Shawn observed.

"Sometimes the land or previous lava flows act as a barrier to the new flow," said April. "Other times, part of the flow slows down and its outside begins to cool into a hard crust. Later on, lava might break through the crust and flow quickly out again."

Shawn chewed thoughtfully on his pencil. "That must make the lava movement really difficult to predict."

As lava cools, it hardens and turns to rock.

You can find a lot of information about past volcanic eruptions by searching online.

"That's why we need all the information we can get," April said. "Now let's make a map of the lava movements since this flow started two months ago. Kayla, can you pull up the observatory's information about that?"

"You got it," Kayla said. She, April, and Reggie helped Shawn color in a blank map of the island. They marked the lava's progress using a different color for each week. Using other maps they found online, they marked the locations where people lived near the flow. Shawn added a big star where April's house was.

Once the map was done, April looked at the clock. "It's getting late," she said. "Why don't we take a break and get back to it in the morning?"

Shawn couldn't stop his yawn. "Good plan," he said.

ALIEN VOLCANOES

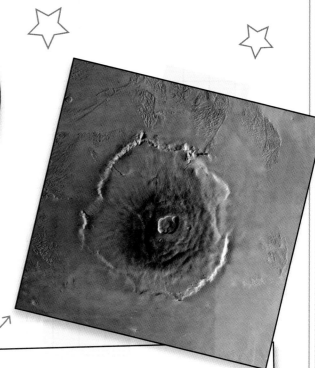

Scientists have not discovered a volcano larger than Olympus Mons.

Earth is not the only place in our solar system with volcanoes. Venus has the most volcanoes of any planet. Scientists have counted more than 1,600 major volcanic features on the planet. There could be as many as a million smaller ones. However, they are thought to be extinct, or no longer active.

Our solar system's largest volcano is the extinct Olympus Mons on Mars. This massive mountain is more than 100 times bigger than Mauna Loa, Earth's largest volcano.

Jupiter's moon Io is the most volcanically active body in our solar system. Saturn's moon Titan might also be volcanically active. Scientists believe Titan may have an unusual feature: "cold" volcanoes. These volcanoes shoot out ice, water, and other materials instead of lava.

Scientists learn about these alien volcanoes by comparing them to Earth's volcanoes. Many of them, including Olympus Mons, are believed to be very similar to Kīlauea and Mauna Loa.

Volcano observatories usually update their Web sites with the latest information as new measurements are taken.

Early the next morning, Shawn and Kayla checked online for any new information on the eruption. They updated their charts. By the time they were finished, April and Reggie had joined them.

"How does it look?" Reggie asked.

"I don't think there's enough sulfur dioxide to worry about right now," answered Shawn. "The lava might be a problem, though. Its speed keeps changing, but the flow hasn't stopped."

"What about earthquakes?"

Kayla dug out the chart on seismograph readings. "Some little ones have happened around Puʻu ʻŌʻō. There have also been some quakes around vents that aren't part of the flow we're looking at. Nothing really big, though."

"So there's a good chance there won't be any really explosive eruptions coming up," said Reggie. "Do you think the flow will stop anytime soon?"

Shawn looked at all the evidence they'd gathered. "I would argue that the lava will come out for a while longer," he said.

April asked them to show her where the lava was heading. Shawn picked up the map. "The lava from Puʻu ʻŌʻō is mostly moving northeast," he said, pointing. "And it sort of spreads out from there. It's already reached some houses."

↑ Violent eruptions near cities and towns can cause serious problems.

Lava can travel a long way under the right conditions.

"So let's assume Shawn is correct and the lava flow continues," April said, then thought for a moment. "Long-lasting flows can widen a lot over time. How far are we from the lava flow right now?"

Kayla pointed at the big star on the map. "We are here. That's maybe 20 miles (32 kilometers) north of where the lava flow is. I doubt the lava will spread that far."

"If it does, it will probably take longer than a few days," Reggie pointed out.

April and Shawn agreed. "It's pretty unlikely we'll be affected by the lava flow anytime soon. But we should be prepared anyway," said April.

"That's our next step, then: an evacuation plan!" Shawn declared.

PREDICTING THE FUTURE

Tornadoes and other natural disasters can completely destroy homes and businesses. →

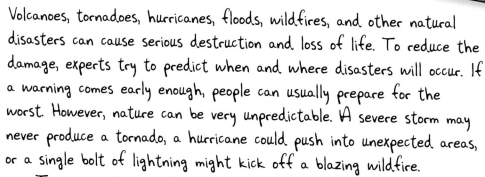

Volcanoes, tornadoes, hurricanes, floods, wildfires, and other natural disasters can cause serious destruction and loss of life. To reduce the damage, experts try to predict when and where disasters will occur. If a warning comes early enough, people can usually prepare for the worst. However, nature can be very unpredictable. A severe storm may never produce a tornado, a hurricane could push into unexpected areas, or a single bolt of lightning might kick off a blazing wildfire.

To improve their predictions, scientists look for patterns in past events. For example, they have learned that the most violent volcanic eruptions happen when a crater is especially deep. Scientists might also notice that a certain kind of storm is more likely to produce a tornado. Maybe they figure out that hurricanes tend to move in a certain way. Or they realize that flash floods are more likely to occur after a wild-fire or when snow melts earlier than usual. The experts then compare these patterns to what is going on around them. If events fit a pattern, the experts can predict that disaster might strike.

CHAPTER 5

AN ESCAPE PLAN

↖ People living near active volcanoes must prepare emergency plans in case of eruptions.

"Lava flows can behave unpredictably, right?" asked Shawn.

April nodded. "We do all we can at the HVO to warn people ahead of time to leave dangerous areas. But the situation can change very quickly and unexpectedly."

"So people might need to evacuate on short notice." Shawn tapped his pencil on his notebook. He wanted to help design the perfect emer-

gency plan for his cousins. There were a lot of details to sort out.

The family discussed options for how to travel and how to keep track of each other. Shawn took notes as everyone talked. Reggie had a car and a cell phone, but Kayla had neither. They also went to different schools that were not close together. April counted off possibilities on her fingers. "Kayla could get a ride with her friends Cory or Dylan if she needed to. And Reggie has his car. But I might have to be on hand at the observatory."

In emergency situations, government or military workers might be sent to help people evacuate areas where a volcano is expected to erupt.

↖ A simple text message is all it takes to let family members know where you are during an emergency.

"We'll communicate with text messages when we can," Reggie said. "That frees the phone lines up for emergency workers. Kayla doesn't have a phone, but we can get the numbers for Kayla's school and Cory's and Dylan's parents."

"I'll probably be back in Kansas by the time anything happens," Shawn said. "You guys can all text me to let me know you're safe. That way, I can help keep track of all of you. Plus you'll always know who to ask for updates. If we need to evacuate while I'm here, we can use my dad as a contact."

← Hawaiʻi's warm weather and sandy beaches attract huge crowds of tourists all year long.

Everyone nodded. Finally, they decided on places to meet in case they were separated. Then they used Shawn's notes to type up their plan. They printed out five copies: one for each person, plus one for the refrigerator door.

"Phew!" exhaled Shawn when it was all finished. "I feel a lot better about the volcano now."

Reggie laughed. "Good. Now why don't we go to the beach?"

"I thought you'd never ask." Shawn said. "As long as it's nowhere near any hot lava!"

THE BAD AND THE GOOD OF VOLCANIC ERUPTIONS

Many islands are formed by undersea volcanic eruptions.

Volcanoes can cause serious problems. Eruptions can kill hundreds or even thousands of people. They can destroy surrounding towns and wildlife. Really big explosions can even bring the entire planet's temperature down a few degrees by filling the **atmosphere** with dust and ash.

However, volcanoes are not all bad. The materials that come out when they erupt help improve the soil. This makes the plants that grow after eruptions healthy. Volcanoes also create new land, from tiny islands in the Pacific Ocean to Earth's huge, ancient continents. Volcanic activity can even be harnessed to provide energy for homes and businesses. More importantly, volcanoes are a source of water on Earth's surface and of gases in its atmosphere. Without volcanoes, we wouldn't have oceans, rivers, or lakes. The air we breathe would be much less breathable.

GLOSSARY

acid rain (AS-id RAYN) rain that has been made acidic by chemicals in the air

atmosphere (AT-muhs-feer) the mixture of gases that surrounds a planet

crater (KRAY-tur) a bowl-shaped formation at the top of a volcano

evacuate (i-VAK-yoo-ayt) to leave an area or building because it is dangerous there

lava flow (LAH-vuh FLOH) a mass or stream of hot, molten rock material on the planet's surface

magma (MAG-muh) hot, molten rock material beneath the earth's surface

observatory (uhb-ZUR-vuh-tor-ee) a building that has instruments for monitoring volcanoes, stars, weather, or other things

satellites (SAT-uh-lites) objects that orbit around Earth, the moon, or another heavenly body

seismograph (SIZE-muh-graf) an instrument that detects and measures earthquakes

tsunamis (soo-NAH-meez) very large, destructive waves caused by an underwater earthquake or volcano

vapor (VAY-pur) the gas that forms from something that is usually a liquid or solid at normal temperatures

vents (VENTS) openings in a volcano through which smoke and lava escape

volcanologist (vul-kuh-NAH-luh-jist) a scientist who studies volcanoes

BOOKS

Rusch, Elizabeth. *Eruption! Volcanoes and the Science of Saving Lives.*
    Boston: Houghton Mifflin Harcourt, 2013.

Star, Fleur. *Look Inside: Volcano.* New York: DK Publishing, 2011.

WEB SITES

U.S. Geological Survey—Hawaiian Volcano Observatory

http://hvo.wr.usgs.gov/

Visit this Web site for the latest information on Hawai'i's volcanoes.

Volcano World—Your World is Erupting— Oregon State University

http://volcano.oregonstate.edu/

Keep up with the latest volcano news, play games, and go on virtual
tours of some of Earth's most interesting volcanoes.

INDEX

ABOUT THE AUTHOR

Jennifer Zeiger lives in Chicago, Illinois, where she writes and edits books for kids.